Introduction:

What if your son or daughter or roommate in college began to show the early signs of schizophrenia setting in? What if they really began to have trouble getting along with others in everyday life marked by more personal conflicts with others? What if they showed signs of fear, doubt, confusion, suspicions, panic, anger, and paranoia in front of you over even seemingly trite matters? Or what if they even began to threaten or show other signs of unwarranted aggression and conflict with others over very trite matters? What if they suddenly withdrew instead of continue to participate in the world at large among us all? What if they seemed far away in terms of where their head is now at, and not in the reality that is common to us all anymore? Just what should a concerned friend or loved one do to help alleviate the potential challenges that this person is beginning to face?

Well the most obvious answer for the immediate is to get one to seek professional help for those with persistent problems in how they think and behave in everyday life before it gets even worse. Now what could really be happening is that they are just going thru a phase in their life that amounts to growing pains and not full-fledged schizophrenia, but at least sometimes mental illness lurks on the horizon for them, so it may be better to be safe than sorry.

The obvious overall remaining question still remains-why did they all of a sudden change the way they behave to something that is very peculiar, weird, and repugnant? What essentially speaking does it really mean to become a schizophrenic? Can this disorder be rationally understood at all or not? Finally, if we knew and understood what schizophrenia entails can we understand its cause, or then how it comes about? I personally am an optimist that believes that we can all at least understand rationally how schizophrenia comes about and further educate the masses accordingly to set us free from this disorder.

My master's thesis is my belief that we should indeed increase education to the masses on the nature of this disorder to help wipe out its devastation to anyone. I really believe that with more education on the nature of this disorder, this should lead to smarter choices by all accordingly to prevent harm to someone from this disorder. Since by now we can rationally understand what schizophrenia is about-delusion, the biggest sub-type of schizophrenia it can be overcome by all. I will now develop in five sections an overall understanding of the nature of this disorder, in order to prevent schizophrenia from continuing to hurt anyone:

First- to educate the masses on what schizophrenia is about we need to know what this substantially means: the definition, the most direct symptoms of it, as well as the potential cause or causes of it.

Second- there are other anxiety disorders that in many cases overlap with schizophrenia that we should be aware of in order to better explain all of the symptoms overall that young people typically experience that are becoming schizophrenic. Just the five most direct symptoms of this disorder all by themselves do not tell you enough about the schizophrenic symptoms that young people may be experiencing. It is important that young people are hip to a fuller understanding than what just the direct symptoms by themselves tell you.

Third- and this is where we get to some original thinking of my own, I emphasize how delusional thinking is a major force and sub-type behind schizophrenia. Delusion is to believe something with conviction that something is the case, even when presented with superior evidence to the contrary. (Others with knowledge about schizophrenia would be more apt to emphasize the other symptoms too more, including and especially hallucination. No doubt hallucination too is a major factor behind schizophrenia, that involves hearing, seeing, tasting, smelling or feeling that which is not real, that also may include a misconstruction of the meaning of the behavior of others at the same time that we call delusion then as well.)

I have to add to this discussion an original diagram of my own that focuses on the very thought process of the steps while entering delusion that highlights the most probable thoughts that one has during the entrance of it. (Believe it or not this diagram allows one to analyze how they might have gotten off the trail of thought that led to being pulled entirely into a delusional state of mind.) In contemporary models of delusion after Conrad, it includes the use of "symbolic meaning" in trying to let's say understand the potential meaning by others in what you initially seen, heard or lets heard about that pertained to their behavior. From there, curiosity and wonderment may take over in this same person, now trying to decide whether they have been sent a message by whomever may be using "symbolic communication" deliberately as a means to do so.

Let's suppose hypothetically that you do decide that the symbolic meaning that came alive to you about whatever was really indeed a message being sent to you by someone else when this is not the case. And then if you were to analyze objectively what this then could be telling you as a result it implies that you are simply not being fully rational because you assumed or then jumped to the false conclusion that this then necessarily means that someone were sending you a message when it's not true. I have much faith in the potential use of my objective tool, my diagram, which puts into perspective the thought process itself entering delusion. If we are to just focus on the logical progression of the thought process while entering delusion, even without the diagram we should be able to assess the same thing if we are to really think about it, however it is much more easily done with the use of my diagram to help us focus more precisely on the particular thoughts that one were having during the entrance of delusion. My diagram then should be considered a quite useful tool to illustrate how the thought process itself can be important and helpful in understanding how one is duped into delusion, so that one just might decide not to be deceived into believing a false

conclusion.

Fourth- I allude to the modern day treatment that is being given to those

diagnosed with schizophrenia. The modern day treatment consists of anti-psychotic

drugs that one must take on a regular basis, but therapy too that includes not only

education to the patient by the doctor about how to cope in general better with their

disorder that by now sometimes includes also personal education on the nature of their

disorder itself. They too may be coached to maintain a positive attitude towards others in

the interest of a faster and complete recovery. They may be told that a positive attitude

towards others makes for a happier, more self-actualized person as well.

Fifth- we really need more education in general on schizophrenia to the masses

that should help significantly prevent delusional thinking among them, and further stop

schizophrenia from hurting our young people to a large degree overall. As part of this

education, a positive attitude not only by the patient of this disorder, but for all of us is

important for success; a positive attitude in general towards others should make all our

lives run smoother.

Demographics for Schizophrenia:

Schizophrenia is a devastating and atrocious-(usually delusion- filled disorder)

that strikes many young people, especially those in their late teens or early twenties.

Who does it strike?

Individuals with schizophrenia are found in every culture, every geographic region of the world, and at all historical periods of time. Incidence of schizophrenia refers to the number of new cases of schizophrenia detected in a given period, and it is most typically stated in terms of an annual incidence rate. The annual incidence rate to industrialized countries, according to a World Health Organization study, is between 16 and 28 cases per 1,000 individuals (or between (1 and 3%), a finding that is consistent over a number of years using different diagnostic procedures across varying conditions (Vandenbos 2000, pp. 161).

At what age do people start experiencing the symptoms of a schizophrenic?

Onset of Schizophrenic symptoms most typically occurs between the ages of 18 and 30 years. Rates of schizophrenia in children and in adolescents is generally low (1 in 10,000 or less), and when it occurs between the age groups it is typically quite severe. Males are somewhat more likely to meet diagnostic criteria for schizophrenia slightly earlier in age than females. The most frequent age range for onset of schizophrenia symptoms for males is 18 to 25 years, whereas for females it is 26 to 45 years. There is no consistent explanation for these differences in age of onset of severe schizophrenic symptomatology. In general age of onset is before age 45 in 75%of the cases of schizophrenia, and age of onset is before 60 years in 90% of cases. (Vandenbos 2000, pp. 161)

Not most of the time but occasionally they may lash out with violence at others, but usually are more inclined to hurt their own self with a suicide attempt as a result.

 The suicide risk: Approximately 5%-6% of individuals with schizophrenia die by suicide, about 20% attempt suicide on one or more occasions, and many more have significant ideation. Suicidal behavior is sometimes in response to command hallucinations to harm oneself or others. Suicide risk remains high over the whole life span for males and females, although it may be high among young males with comorbid substance use. Other risk factors include having depressive symptoms or felling of hopelessness and being unemployed, and the risk is higher, also in this period after a psychotic episode of hospital discharge. (DSM 5, 2013, pp.104)

Part I What is a Schizophrenic?

 A. Definition of a Schizophrenic

 First we need to ask ourselves what is schizophrenia?

"Most individual encountering a person with schizophrenia will recognize that person as quite strange and very different, at least during the acute phase. Such patient appear "out of touch" with reality, in that they behave in highly atypical ways. They verbalize ideas and beliefs that seem bizarre, they exhibit strange and dramatic behaviors: and they manifest unexpected emotion. It is common to feel confused, uncomfortable, and perhaps frightened when interacting with a person with schizophrenia, because they seem to be living in, and responding to a world that operates on principles quite different from those of most other people. (Vandenbos, 2000, pp. 161)

According to Schizophrenia Symptoms, Signs, and Coping Tips by Jeannie Segal and Melinda Smith "Schizophrenia is a brain disorder that affects the way a person behaves, thinks, and see the world. The most common form is paranoid schizophrenia, or schizophrenia have an altered perception of reality. They may see or hear things that don't exist, speak in strange or confusing ways, believe that others are trying to harm them, or feel like they're constantly watched." (Smith and Segal, 2017, pp.1) Another way of saying this same thing is that a schizophrenic is simply not in reality with what they believe to be the case about others. There are those that think that schizophrenia is the "doctor Jeckyl-Mr. Hyde syndrome" in someone's behavior, or that it is thinking out-loud to yourself when no one is around but this is not always necessarily the case. It is really when they are not seeing an accurate picture of what is really going on around them, this then takes them away from reality as it is understood by normal people.

B. Symptoms of a Schizophrenic

According to the DSM-5 there are 5 certain particular symptoms of schizophrenia that one could be said to very directly show when acquiring schizophrenia. If one were to have two or more of these symptoms for over the course of a month- then one could be said to be suffering from schizophrenia. These include: 1) Delusions 2) Hallucinations 3)

Disorganized speech (e.g., frequent derailment or incoherence). 4) Grossly disorganized

or catatonic behavior. 5) Negative symptoms (i.e., diminished emotional expression or

avolition).   Also according to Melinda Smith and Jeanie Segal's *Schizophrenic

Symptoms, Signs, and Coping Tips,* it also lists these same five symptoms for establishing

what the criteria is for this disorder. (Smith and Segal 2017, pp.3-6). It also adds

particular description about each one of them that also sheds keen insight on each one of

them.

1. According to Melinda Smith and Jeanie Segal,

    "A delusion is a firmly held idea that a person has despite clear and obvious

    evidence that it isn't true. Delusions are extremely common in schizophrenia,

    occurring in more than 90% of those who have the disorder. Often these

    delusions involve illogical or bizarre ideas or fantasies…"

        A delusion in most cases usually entails believing a falsehood about the

    true meaning of the behavior of others because your thoughts misconstrued the

    true meaning of why they did what they did.

2. According to Melinda Smith and Jeanie Segal,

        "Hallucinations are sounds or other sensations experienced as real when

    they exist only in your mind. While hallucinations can involve any of the five

    senses, auditory hallucinations (e.g. hearing voices or some other sound) are the most common in schizophrenia, often occurring when you misinterpret your own inner self-talk as coming form an outside source."

So now when one listens to one's own thoughts and then mistakes them for someone else talking to you this is an example of the most major kind of hallucination. One could of course still see, feel, taste, or smell something that is also not real.

3. According to Melinda Smith and Jeanie Segal on disorganized speech-

"Schizophrenia can cause you to have trouble concentrating and maintaining a train of thought, extremely manifesting itself in the way that you speak. You may respond to queries with an unrelated answer, start sentences with one topic and somewhere completely different, speak incoherently, or say illogical things."

Whereas I am definitely not believing that we all don't at least from time to time have a slight falling way from our best speaking, to continually show paranoia that disrupts our speech can be a sign many times of real trouble within.

4. According to Melinda Smith and Jeanie Segal on disorganized behavior-

"Disorganized behavior include Schizophrenia disrupts goal-directed activity, impairing your ability to take care of yourself, your work, and interact with others."

Disorganized behavior of course-especially when it all the time could be an inward sign of confusion or serious distress.

5. According to Melinda Smith and Jeanie Segal on negative symptoms,

"The so-called "negative' symptoms of schizophrenia refer to the absence of normal behaviors found in healthy individuals, such as, Lack of emotion expression; lack of interest or enthusiasm; Seeming lack of interest in the world; speech difficulties and abnormalities."

When you stop and think about it practically all of the signs of negativity that become this particular schizophrenic symptom it could reveal an attitude that one does not care about one's self or others anymore like they should. To withdraw from others and no longer care about yourself reflect a negative attitude that we should be wary of. Of course one must be careful not to jump to false conclusions about the true meaning of why someone would begin to spend more time alone. It could be that this same person is becoming a real thinker and writer on their own for example, and really need to spend more time alone with their thoughts to be able to grow in this regard. Even if this is the case it may take time to convince others that this person is really o.k. if since they now spend a lot of time alone, and to worry about them is understandable.

C. Causes of Schizophrenia

Next we need to ask ourselves what is the cause of schizophrenia? First, could it be that this disease is biologically caused? Second, could it be that this disease is genetically caused and/or carried? Third, could schizophrenia be directly or indirectly related to the environment and/or social situation that one finds one's self in? For instance does unemployment in itself really cause schizophrenia? Does social anxiety on the job or at school lead to schizophrenia? Do the psychological changes in general that one goes thru in high school and especially college age contribute to the "freak-out" that schizophrenia becomes? Fourth, could a language or cultural barrier break down trust and understanding between people that should be able to be established where the accusation to the victim of this is to be labeled? Does the stigmatization of the public for those who are mentally handicapped heighten within them the symptoms of this disorder? Is Schizophrenia race related? Fifth, could schizophrenia actually really be seen as just a metaphor that is derogatory name calling to all socially undesirables in general as opposed to a real illness?

First, as it pertains to the biological angle for understanding schizophrenia there right now happens to be solid belief among a broad range in the scientific community that they have proof that indeed schizophrenia is biologically caused. "Neuropsychiatric studies using modern brain imaging techniques are rapidly redefining schizophrenia. Physical and chemical changes found in the brain have largely discredited beliefs that environmental attachment, family interactions, or stress cause schizophrenia." (Taylor 1987, pp. 115)

Right now they apparently have considerable proof that the brains frontal and temporal lobes and limbic system just may be responsible for the development of schizophrenia. Taylor (1987, pp. 115) notes:

"Research on schizophrenia is focusing on the brain's frontal and temporal

lobes and limbic system. The limbic system is a relatively small area that includes

the hypothalamus, amygdala, skeptical, and hippocampal regions. The frontal lobe,

together, with the limbic system, is responsible for receiving, organizing, selecting

generally making sense of both internal and external perceptions. Damage to the

limbic system of animals produces inappropriate behavior, visual screening

problems, and emotional changes. The evidence indicates that "abnormalities in the

limbic system of human beings may produce…distortions of perceptions, illusions,

hallucinations, feelings of depersonalization, paranoia, and catatonic like

behaviors….in short, the symptoms of schizophrenia.

Whereas this discovery is thought to be a major break thru and victory for those

who believe that schizophrenia is really biologically caused, it definitely does not give

what I believe to be a full account of what they are really just beginning to understand.

Look even if you were to pinpoint that part of the brain namely the frontal lobes and

limbic system where this part of your brain controls this particular cognitive function of

your thinking this still does not tell us that we can necessarily then cure schizophrenia

with this information as a result.

Second is schizophrenia genetically caused or carried? We definitely at this point

do not have the proof that schizophrenia is necessarily directly caused by the gene pattern

itself that one has, but at the same time if there are individuals in your family with this disorder, that there is an increased likelihood of someone in the next generation on down with the same blood line of getting schizophrenia. "The genetic factor in schizophrenia has been underscored by recent findings that first- degree biological relatives of schizophrenics are 10 times more likely to develop the disorder than are members of the general population." (Fallon, 2013, pp.27) This can be important and useful to know, so that like when we see the opening signs of it in someone that if it carries more in your family tree to be extra careful to get medical care for example when a person in the next generation down in the same family is suffering from schizophrenic symptoms.

The third potential cause for schizophrenia that we should be aware of is the environmental, social, and psychological factors in one's life that includes the stress we take on every day and potentially hidden trauma in one's life. First of all I for one am not convinced that to claim biological factors alone tells the whole story about what could actually make schizophrenia become real in people.   I am believing that there are definitely environmental, social, and psychological factors too that at the very least trigger this disorder to come alive in someone, even if it may not turn out to be the most ultimate cause behind it. There is a lot of change that is going on in one's life from the time of high school thru college age. When you leave high school you are thrust into a more difficult student role and/ or are learning a job role that you may feel inadequate for. The subsequent stress that we experience from these change in our life is real and affects our thinking.

For instance, one may develop social anxiety on the job or at school on a higher level related to new participation around other people. Social anxiety happens to be the fear of being judged by others- usually under stressful circumstances like in a speech contest at school or on the job in new or difficult role! The fear in social anxiety is provoked by the environment itself. "The social situations almost always provoke fear or anxiety" (DSM, 2013, pp. 107) This means that you will be concerned about how you are perceived by others in a very real and direct way when you are around others. "Social anxiety" itself is definitely not schizophrenia, as schizophrenia almost always includes delusion or hallucination very directly speaking to be considered such. But now add paranoid false beliefs about others too in addition to social anxiety in general and it may very well get the label schizophrenia by a trained psychiatrist. This of course would be evidence that proves that with other direct symptoms of schizophrenia present like delusion in someone, that already has "social anxiety", it might very well lead to the label schizophrenic to describe this person.

Unemployment too in particular many times breeds discontentment- especially when this means ones' overall income will then be reduced making it tougher to pay the bills and keep a roof over your head. Unemployment sometimes turns into a negative attitude of hate for the system unto delusional proportions. The fact that you may be spending more time alone too will affect your thinking, perhaps negatively.

In a recent study twenty-one people with Serious Mental Illness (SMI) were interviewed that were either employed or unemployed.   Not all of the people that were in the study really wanted to even be working according to it, but at least some of the people that were in it reported an upswing in their social relationships with others when they got back to work . (Saavedra, Lopez, Gonzales, and Cubero, 2016, pp. 511)

Does work help recovery?

Most of the people interviewed mentioned that their work experience had a significant effect on their identity and also on the way that others looked at them. In particular, six participants mentioned very important changes in the image transmitted to other significant people thanks to employment. The positive assessment of employment as a means of identity construction goes beyond the most intensive illnesses in the people who are unemployed or have not been working for long (Saavedra, Lopez, Gonzales, and Cubero, 2016, pp.511)

This is at least some proof that there is a direct correlation between the symptoms of (SMI) related to unemployment, and how then a new chance for employment can change this for the better. And finally then, the environmental and social situation that one find's oneself in, including the psychological changes that one is going thru can be seen as an overall viable factor for understanding what causes schizophrenia.

Fourth, Cross Cultural barriers in the United Sated could be said to exist in mental illness treatment for those of another culture, race, or ethnicity. According to the surgeon General cross-cultural barriers to seeking help can be classified in four categories: cognitive, affective, value orientation, and physical or structural. First, an example of cognitive differences in culture would be the fact that we give mental illness therapy for what in their culture you would instead receive help from a medical physical doctor for psychological problems. Second, affective barriers have to do with the unwillingness to seek help for mental illness by those from other cultures now living in our society, because of the stigma and shame associated that goes along with it from their own viewpoint. Third, value orientation barriers pertain to the emotional expressions and communication styles, which are particularly relevant to psychotherapy in our culture that is individualistic as opposed to the collectivistic values of their culture. Fourth, barriers exist- the social class or the actual structures of how the system is set up may inhibit minorities from acquiring mental health treatment that they should have access to. These barriers can be seen as allowing schizophrenia to develop in those of another culture that are trying to assimilate into our society. (Leong and Kalibatseva, 2011, PP.2-5)

I have great faith that with people working together in the system we can overcome all of these barriers: First we can find ways to treat those of another culture with the right psychiatric help in doctor care like we have been getting; Second, we can personally encourage another culture to seek help when they need it, informing them that there is no shame in itself with seeing psychiatric doctor; Third, we should train all of our psychiatrists to be sensitive to the cultural differences of a person of another culture when treating them; Fourth, use the system to make laws that forbid discrimination barring those of another social class or race from receiving adequate psychological help.

Then finally the fifth and final proposed causal factor for schizophrenia we should mention here is that schizophrenia is really a metaphor and not a mental illness at all. Szasz's rationale for that belief is that schizophrenia is not really a brain disease, based on objective medical evidence, but really made up.

In 1961, the psychiatrist Thomas Szasz published The Myth of Mental Illness, declaring that unlike physical illness, mental illness is mythological in nature, and we can only speak of the mind being sick in metaphorical terms. Szasz also highlighted the way in which individuals diagnosed as mentally ill were often treated coercively, claiming the psychiatrists acted as agents of social control to deal with deviant moral behavior. (Counter and Spillane, 2017. pp.151)

Szasz argued that (a) illness affects only the body (by definition); (b) the mind" is really the brain or a brain process, (c) therefore, the "mind" cannot be diagnosed on the basis of objective medical signs; (d) therefore mental illness is a myth (e) If the "mind" is really the brain or a brain process (f) then mental illnesses are really brain illnesses. (g) Brain illnesses are the basis of subjective moral criteria; (i) therefore, mental illnesses are diagnosed on the basis of subjective moral criteria; (i) therefore "mental illness" is an oxymoron; (j) so "minds" can only be sick, in the way that jokes are said to be "sick". (Counter and Spillane, 2017,

pp.151)

"It should be emphasized that Szasz never questioned the status of legitimate

brain diseases, such as Alzheimer's or epilepsy, but argued that mental illnesses are

at best metaphorical illnesses and, at worse, egregious fictions. In short, legitimate

illnesses are discovered; illegitimate illnesses are invented. (Counter and Spillane,

2017, pp. 151))

One more thing that should be emphasized about what sounds like a very liberal

understanding of mental illness though is that in actuality Szasz at the same time takes a

critical positon to legal orthodoxy. "Szasz argued that regardless of a diagnosis of mental

illness, individuals are 'always responsible for their conduct" (Counter, P, Spillane, R.,

2017, pp.151)

Now even if one does not take altogether seriously some Thomas Szasz's beliefs

on schizophrenia, as his work is not highly accepted by now anyways, he does indeed

make an important point that to label someone a schizophrenic can sometimes be seen as

just name calling to them because of their low social statis or skin color. This is

important because sometimes false diagnosis- where someone did not really have a

serious mental disorder were still labeled a schizophrenic nonetheless based on a

potentially biased diagnosis. (A word of caution I would like to spread to those who

don't believe in schizophrenia I am going to tell you right here and now that we should realize schizophrenia has the quality of a "real disorder" that puts one outside reality that

the rest of us are experiencing. Schizophrenia is dangerous and real, and not to be seen

as contingent upon a bigoted attitude by others. We need to pay attention to the

symptoms of a schizophrenic and not just ignore this, for the safety and well-being of all

including those who suffer from it.)

(One more thing I wanted to add on this topic is that whether there is a really a

ultimate biological cause or not behind schizophrenia, stress and shock from all of the

changes in the environment, social arrangement, and the psychological change in general

that one could be said to be going thru at this age is relevant for understanding the

disorder of schizophrenia. To know more about the social situation, environmental

relationship or psychological state of mind at this age should help one understand better

why schizophrenia possibly came alive in them. If we just wait for a complete medical

cure for schizophrenia by itself we just might be waiting around forever for significant

enough improvement from this disorder, whereas if we examine the environmental,

social, and psychological aspects of this disorder we should be well on our way to ending

delusion entirely.)

Part II Disorder

Developing Disorder

It is a fast-paced hurried world where it is sometimes hard to keep pace with everything you set out to, even when you are trying to do you're very best. Young people at high school age or beyond are on a journey of self- discovery in which they could begin to change a lot in terms of their personal identity. By college age when your young people graduate from high school, and then are usually either working full time or going to college much of the time now not living at home but out on their own in many cases. They are playing new roles and are in a process of development as a person. They are in a new environment with different people and the 'name of the game" may by far different then what it once was. All this means that they will be going thru a lot of "psychological change" inside.

It is not surprising that by college age many of them find themselves sitting in a mental health counselor's office receiving advice or coaching on how to deal with the new stress that they are taking on at this juncture in their life. This of course is not necessarily any shame, but should be seen as possibly just the help that you need at this time in your life. They may be experiencing everything from depression, to scopophobia to social anxiety to panic attacks, or even delusion or hallucination that sometimes lead to full- fledged schizophrenic or bipolar. You might say that it is "getting away from them sometimes" as to knowing how to act or cope with the present situation that they are faced with.

Several Disorders that Interrelate with Schizophrenia

Schizophrenia is a disorder! As I have already mentioned schizophrenia is a psychotic disorder that consists of at least two or more of the five most basic symptoms that we find within the schizophrenic spectrum for at least a month. These five symptoms that make up the schizophrenic spectrum once again include delusion, hallucination, disorganized, speech, disorganized behavior, and negative symptoms. There are in fact though other very particular specific "disorders" that sometimes interrelate and overlap with these five symptoms that are already established in the schizophrenic spectrum. They give us a broader perspective on what schizophrenia or psychosis in general could be said to sometimes include. They are paranoia, scopophobia, social anxiety, panic attacks, and obsessive compulsive behavior. I wish to address each one of these same disorders individually and tell you how they could sometimes be said to overlap with those five found in the original schizophrenic spectrum. I will then re-address hallucination and delusion to discuss individually one at a time along with these other disorders just mentioned, as they too both constitute a disorder in themselves, and also are a major factor for establishing the disorder of

schizophrenia.

1. Paranoia, or Paranoid Ideation

First, I wish to discuss the concept of "paranoia" and "paranoid ideation."

"Paranoia is a unfounded or exaggerated mistrust of others sometimes reaching

delusional proportions" (Psychology Dictionary) The kind of fear that this entails can be

said to be heightened and unnatural as opposed to being just everyday worrying about

whatever. Then too there is the expression "paranoid ideation", which really too says

something about the kind of unnatural fear that a paranoid-possesses, or paranoia in

progress. Paranoid ideation is, "cognitive processes of continual suspicion and non-

delusional beliefs of being persecuted, tormented, or treated in an unfair manner by other

people." (Psychology Dictionary) This is in effect to believe that others are mistreating

you. Paranoia or paranoid ideation is definitely a symptom of a paranoid schizophrenic.

It is not difficult to see how the environment and the particular social arrangement there

where you work, live, or commit leisure might be thought to interrelate with the kind of

fears or suspicions that you might have. A friendlier environment of people might get one

to feel more confident instead of one where you feel rejected and unloved by others, but

sometimes one acquire paranoia or paranoid ideation to the point one is literally that way

all the time no matter where they might be under any circumstances.

2. Scopophobia

Scopophobia is morbid fear of being stared at. (Medical Dictionary) Scopophobia is a unnatural fear that you have of being watched that can extend to a potential imagination that you are being observed from the other side of a camera- or even being stalked personally in the same environment that you presently find yourself in.   This particular disorder is really a little bit more common than what someone might realize among the masses, as it is frequently joked about in rock folklore to the point that it says something about the common place of this disorder.   In a popular song by Mike Jackson it says "I always feel like somebody's watching me stop playing tricks on me" I always feel like somebody's watching me, and I have no privacy. In a Hall-N-_Oats song it says, "private eyes their watching you they see your every move. Private eyes their watching you, watching you, watching you…." Yet in another song by Men At Work it says, "who can it be knockin' at my door, go away don't come round here no more…" Then too there is a song by the cars that goes, "You think you're in the movies, but I think that your wild-you might think I'm foolish all I want is you" Yet one more song by Paul Simon called Paranoia Blues- the chorus of which goes, "I've got the paranoia blues from knockin' around in New York city where they roll you for a nickel and they stick you for the extra dime. Anyway you choose you're bound to loose in New York City. Well I just go out in the nick of time. Well I just go out in the nick of time."   (The last two songs just alluded to by Men at Work and by Paul Simon are both examples of songs emphasize paranoia itself along with a scopophobic emphasis to it that people are really staring at you.

In literature too this theme of scopophobia also pops up. For example in Ernest Hemingway novels in particular several of Hemingway's characters could be said to have a scopophobic outlook or perspective on reality.

Another way to think about the existence of scopophobia among the masses is to also emphasize how it is the case that when one is scopophobic one also might feel like they are elevated to a "stage performance in what they do just in everyday life. According to William Shakespeare, the great play-right, "the world is like a stage and we are all the men and women of the play… the actors on it……." This is proof to me anyways that William Shakespeare himself thought that we could in fact perceive all our actions out in the real world as a stage act that where we are performer. Then too Erwin Goffman, a renowned thinker in psychology in the twentieth century also thought that our everyday actions that we commit out in the real world everyday could also be seen as a performance or stage act in which we are like performers on a stage. Goffman declares at the very opening of his book The Presentation of Self In Everyday Life, in the introduction:

When an individual enters the presence of others, they commonly seek to acquire information about him or to bring into play information about him already possessed. They will be interested in his general socio-economic status, his conception of self, his attitudes toward them his competence, his trustworthiness, etc. Although some of this information seems to be quite practical reason for acquiring it. Information about the individual help to define the situation, enabling others to know in advance what he will expect of them and what they may expect of him. Informed in these ways, the others will know how best to act in order to call forth a desired response from him. …

In other words, the whole world can be our judge deciding how well we put on a performance for them in everyday life in all that we do. From there, it is not hard to see how young people experiencing a "scopophobic" state of mind, where it may feel like all eyes are upon you- may also feel like they are elevated to a stage performance in front of others in all that they do. It really may seem to this same person that a camera is on them and that really indeed are giving a stage performance to others.

(No doubt in some sense scopophobia obviously could be said to be environmentally related sometimes, but sometimes this fear is real for someone no matter where they go. To say that the environment or the social situation that they were in could be said to be related to the problem though definitely could be said to have potential viability.) There really happens to be no known cause for this disorder, but by virtue of the fact that a lot of people-even normal people, feel sometimes like a stage act one could theorize that it is really just part of a stage of psychological development that anyone that is enlightened has experienced along the way to one degree or another.

3. Social Anxiety

Next we need to consider "social anxiety". "Generally speaking social anxiety is the fear of being evaluated by others. Social anxiety is a "marked fear or anxiety about one or more social situations in which the individual is exposed to possible scrutiny by others. Examples include social interactions, being observed, and performing in front of others." (DSM-5, 2013,pp. 202) For example you could be said to have social anxiety if you are now working in a group situation of a now kind that requires a lot of work related communication toward your co-workers that you are having a difficulty delivering on due to past inhibitions in your interactions with others. Then too for an example you could be thrust into a situation at school where it is your job to deliver a speech when you have no practice speaking in front of a whole group of people and you are terribly reserved and shy in your communication with others.

It is important to remember that the presence of this disorder in someone does not then necessarily make this same person a schizophrenic too as this may be far from true. Many people have social anxiety that do not also have schizophrenia even though these two disorders could be said to sometimes interact with each other. And if for example one has extreme fear of others that is also accompanied by delusion or hallucination too then they then could possibly be said to be schizophrenic too.

4. Panic Attacks

Next we need to discuss panic attack or then panic disorder. Stated in the DSM-5:

A panic attack is an abrupt surge of intense fear or intense discomfort that reaches a peak within minutes, and during which time four or more of a list of 13 physical and cognitive symptoms occur. The symptoms of a panic attack include (1) Palpitations, pounding heart, or accelerated heart rate. (2) Sweating (3 Trembling or shaking. (4)

Sensations of shortness of breath or smothering. (5) Feeling of choking. (6) Chest

pain or discomfort. (7) Nausea or abdominal distress (8) Feeling dizzy, unsteady,

light-headed, 0r faint. (9) Chills or heat sensations. (10) Paresthesias (numbing or

tingling sensations. (11) Derealization (feelings of unreality) or depersonalization

(being detached from oneself). (12) Fear of losing control or "going crazy." (13)

Fear of dying. (DSM-5 2013 pp.208)

There is definitely too sometimes a connection between a panic attack, where you

get emotionally shook-up about something, and then perhaps react with a fit of anger

about whatever. Like the coach of a baseball or football team where when the coach

think that a bad call has been made which will hurt his team's opportunity to win let's say

that in an actual state of panic now coupled with anger he or her may bitch vehemently

about the call in question right then and there. To yell out-loud about whatever that

bothers you of course can sometimes be a manifestation of a panic attack that is possibly

getting carried away. A drunken rage could too I suppose under certain circumstances be

considered part of a panic attack too when fear and panic take over inside of someone.

And as to whether this makes you a schizophrenic or not it definitely could be said to be

going in that direction.

It is important to keep in mind that just because one has panic attacks does not

then mean necessarily that this same person is schizophrenic, but this is quite possible.

Anxiety, at the very least is definitely present when a panic attack occurs in someone. "Anxiety is considered an expected symptom of psychosis, which is accountable for psychotic disorders." (CHING-YEN, MD, CHIA-YIH LI, MD AND YONG-YI YANG MD, 2001, pp. 55) Then too there is definitely the possibility that delusion is going on in the mind of those that are easy to get angry; like they maybe are really misconstruing the general meaning or the overall purpose in the issue.

5. OCD or Obsessive Compulsive Disorder

Obsessive compulsive disorder includes the presence of obsessions and compulsion both. Obsessions are: "Recurrent and persistent thoughts, urges, or images that are experienced, at some cause marked anxiety or distress." (DSM-5 2013, pp. 237) Compulsion is: "Repetitive behaviors (e.g., hand washing, ordering, checking, or mental act (e.g. praying, counting, repeating words silently) that the individual feels driven to perform in response to an obsession or according to rules that must be applied rigidly." (DSM-5 2013, pp. 237) Pace walking back and forth continuously or chain smoking everyday are no doubt examples of obsessive compulsive behavior. Without claiming to know for sure why people become an obsessive compulsive person beyond just to say that they at the same time suffering "addiction" to cigarettes, alcohol, or whatever. There is also sometimes a direct enough connection between do believe too in general that obsessive compulsive behavior many times has something to do with the wrestles-ness or wrestle-less energy that we may be said to have at a young age. This we can train ourselves to channel constructively. Believe it or not there is a much more potentially happy ending that can come out of wrestle- less energy when it is channeled constructively instead of for something pointless or negative. Let's imagine taking our wrest-less energy that we may have in our youth and instead of using it for something negative use it for something positive and see how much better this works for you. A classic example of this would be a young person that instead of chain smoking goes long distance running instead and sheds pounds and then wins a race too. What too about a young mechanic who instead of just sits in the house in the evening making one trip after the next to the refrigerator to get another and another and another beer he instead goes back out to the garage behind his houses after and becomes the best mechanic in the town? We can indeed learn to channel our wrestle –less energy constructively if we put our mind to it.

There is of course the possibility that our OCD is intertwined with delusional thinking that like a "bad habit" in itself is something not to like. If one's wrest-less energy is connected to an "obsession" that is "compulsive" that also is based on a "negative fantasy" that misconstrue a real picture of reality this could be dangerous and definitely be said to be a schizophrenic tendency then.

6. Hallucination

Next I wish to briefly discuss hallucination. As we have already discussed, "Hallucinations are sounds or other sensations experienced as real when they exist only in your mind." (Smith, M., and Segal, J., 2017, pp.4). Once again hallucination like

delusion is directly speaking a schizo-type disorder.   Hallucination is of course one of

the five original symptoms of this Process disorder. Hallucination like delusion is a

"major symptom" of this disorder sometimes, as it can take people out of reality as the

rest of us understand it.

7. Delusion

Once again, "A delusion is a firmly held idea that person has despite clear and

obvious evidence that it isn't true. Delusions are extremely common in schizophrenia,

occurring in more than 90% of those who have the disorder. Often these delusions

involve illogical or bizarre ideas or fantasies…" (Smith, M., and Segal, J., 2017, pp.4).

Delusion is to believe with conviction that something is true, even when it is not and you

have been presented with much better evidence to the contrary. Dorothy Ruiz, a

prominent researcher on schizophrenia, says in effect that "schizophrenia is delusion"! A

quote directly from her says, "Schizophrenia is an illusive illness. The symptoms

consists of persecution or reference not occurring in the context of severe depression;…"

(Ruiz, D., 1982. pp 315)

(Two of the most common kinds of delusion that one could be said to believe (1)

a delusion of persecution and (2) the delusion of reference. First, a persecution delusion

is a "belief that others, often a vague "they" are out to get them" (Smith, M., and Segal,

J., 2017, pp.4). A persecution delusion is a very common kind of delusion that is quite wide-spread among the young people all over the world. A persecution delusion really tricks one's own mind into believing that others are against them when this simply may not be the case. This of course is dangerous not only to the one that suffers this particular kind of delusion, but could of course potentially be harmful to others that they think they are out to harm them when it is just not the case.   Another very common kind of delusion that sometimes interrelates and overlaps with a persecution delusion is the delusion of reference that could be said to incorporate "ideas of reference" that happen not to be true. The delusion of reference (ideas of reference) is "a neutral environmental event is believed to have special and personal meaning." (Smith, M., and Segal, J., 2017, pp. 4) If let's say you interpret what is actually frivolous in meaning in how others behave to have special meaning, where you think that they are trying to send you message when it's not the case- this could be said to be the delusion of reference. This of course could have very negative consequences for themselves or others that we don't want or need. Delusion and hallucination is the most major symptoms in what actually puts one's mind "out of reality" to get that same person labeled a schizophrenic.)

Experiences of Youth

All young people of course experience "growing pains" as they grow up. O.K., now what is the difference between the kind of growing pains that typifies what just anybody might experience growing up, and those that get labeled a schizophrenic? Don't we all get sad, lonely or frustrated sometimes? And didn't we all feel radically incomplete for many tasks as adolescents, where we have to learn to improve in our

ability to reason and follow instructions and/or procedures more effectively? Didn't we

all for sure make at least small mistakes in general along the way?   But do we all

however all overreact and/or run from our circumstances with an altogether negative

interpretation of others? Did we all necessarily imagine that frivolous movements in

other people's behavior meant that we were being sent a message from them? Did we all

imagine that other are against us and/or out to get us because of mild differences of

opinion?   Did we all project a fantasy in our "mind's eye of what we then believe is

going in the environment right in front of us like ghosts of people that are really not

there? Altogether it is the case that symptoms of schizophrenia including delusion and

hallucination advance in some, while others do not venture as far into a non-real fantasy

about others as much.

A List of the Developing Schizophrenic Symptoms

The following is a list displaying many potential symptoms of behavior that might

be said to relate with schizophrenia:

The Adolescent Experience or the Symptoms of a Schizophrenic:

(1) Being On a Stage - A lot of young people feel like they are the center of attention or like
an actor on a stage to perform, but it is when young people have abnormal fear associated
with being watched and/or they become delusional- the delusion of reference or a
persecution delusion in particular foremost, that they then become schizophrenic.

(2) Sensing criticism from others without proof. When one is extremely fearful that they are
always being talked about behind their back negatively- where they too develop a

runaway imagination in this regard, this can sometimes be seen as a schizophrenic symptom.

(3) Misinterpretations of bodily sensations- Imagining that you experienced your ears popped, or your skin electronic shocked with electronic equipment from the government, when it was really only from natural causes that we could decipher-this can then be seen as delusion or even schizophrenia itself.

(4) Thinking that others are sending you a message with their behavior in the same environment, mirrored by their behavior in the form of a hint, innuendo, insinuation, or pun with this is just not the case- When this happens this is called the delusion of reference which is definitely a schizophrenic symptom.

(5) Paranoid Mistrust and a Sense of Conspiracy- Whereas it is normal to sometimes be wary of others -just anyone up to a point-especially someone we don't know can be quite normal,
but to think that others in everyday life are out to get them over nothing at all can sometimes be a persecution delusion which is a schizophrenic symptom.

(6) Thinking that you know what is going on behind your back by using psychic phenomena, when you possess no psychic phenomena and are wrong about what you think to be the case-this definitely constitutes delusion that is indeed a schizophrenic symptom

(7) You attribute to others what you are responsible for yourself even though this is obviously not the case- Attribution, where we blame others for what we are responsible for can be done simply as a lie of convenience or ignorance of the facts, but when our attribution is based on delusional thoughts- (where we really misperceived the motive and intent of others let's say) this can then be seen as a schizophrenic symptom or perhaps even tendency.

8) Giving up   - when we give up on life and withdraw from others based on a misinterpretation of the meaning of others behavior in regards to ourselves then this can be said to be as an opening schizophrenic symptom.

(9) Taking Things Personally- It is a tendency among many of the young people to almost take   things personally in terms of how they understand the meaning of the behavior of others, but when we don't grow out of taking things personal when it is not appropriate it sometimes could be said to be related to delusion- and the label "schizophrenic" may be appropriate.

In all honesty, delusion and hallucination too, I know to be more widespread among the population than what most people are aware of though. This is based on, just for one, the fact that a lot of people have to see a psychiatric doctor or counselor for bad nerves that include potential personality clashes with others that may not get labeled schizophrenic, but definitely show at least opening signs of going down that road. I definitely don't buy into the theory that there is more than just 2% of the people that could be said to be outside of reality in their thoughts process. I believe it to be the case, based on evidence that reveals many millions of people have one or more of these other five disorders that we just discussed: paranoia, scopophobia, social anxiety, panic attacks and obsessive compulsive behavior that is sometimes coupled with delusion or hallucination either one that then usually link it to schizophrenia too. An imaginary or distorted picture of reality is created in the minds of perhaps many millions more people than what actually get labeled a schizophrenic. Disorder in general that is directly or indirectly related to schizophrenia is quite widespread among the young people, as they are still growing into a fully enlightened competent adult. They may be paranoid of others; they may be jumping to false conclusions about the intended meaning of the behavior others; they may even think that there is a conspiracy against them by others when this is not true. They may lack patience and tolerance and have social anxiety or even panic attacks that carry them away from reality. They may be an obsessive compulsive person with a truly fantastic notion of how one should go about their business. Look the mind can get "sick" or "lost" along the way to one degree or another while growing up, but let's not give up on each other. Let's keep routing for each other

to be psychologically healthy –fully plugged into reality and fully self-actualized like we

should be.

Part III Delusion

How Many Different Kinds of Delusion Could There Be Said to Be?

There are many, many different kinds of delusions that could be said to exist. Everything from a "persecution delusion" to an "Internet delusion", but for our purposes there are four that are important enough to briefly address individually: (1) the delusion of persecution (2) the delusion of reference (3) the delusion of thought control (4) the delusion of grandeur. First the delusion of persecution is the belief that others are against you, and are out to get you. Second, the delusion of reference is to ascribe special meaning to what one sees in the same environment. (This definitely should be thought to include how we construe the intended meaning the behavior of others in the same environment). Third, the delusion of thought control could be said to be the belief that others are somehow magically controlling your thought process to get you to think or act in a certain particular way. Fourth, the delusion of grandeur is where you think that you are a supernatural being with supernatural power. (Smith, M., Segal, J., 2017, pp. 4)

(As I have already mentioned in Delusion in Part II, two of the most common kinds of delusion for one to experience is the delusion of persecution and then the delusion of reference, which in some cases could be said to overlap with each other. These two delusions will become particularly important in this third section called delusion, especially when I discuss the "mechanics of delusion" itself or "traumatic" experience.)

The History of Delusion in Schizophrenia

Next, we need to discuss briefly the history of the research on schizophrenia, particularly as it pertains to delusion to understand what it has really been about since the origin of the word itself delusion was first invented. We will see how this concept has been modified over time to include a rational understanding of its nature. We will also become acutely aware that the contemporary understanding of delusion just for one really gets to the point more in terms of the steps used to describe and explain the entrance of delusion in someone that is falling prey to it! To study the best researchers on this topic makes for a potentially much better overall understanding of what this disorder should be thought to mean as this concept developed over time.

Jasper

Let's next take the actual excursion down history lane to look at the development of this concept delusion including how we perceive delusion from the beginning of this field of study starting with Karl Jasper at the beginning of the twentieth century. Karl Jasper one of the earliest researchers on schizophrenia, defined a most major symptom of this disorder as delusion. As it pertains to delusion there are four overall major concepts that I wish to share with you that are believe in by Jasper. First, for Jasper there are three criteria in the definition of a delusion that make it a delusion after all, as opposed to just an assumption that just happens to be false. They are conviction, irrefutability and incorrigibility. All three of these attributes are necessary according to Jasper to then call it a delusion: A. We are passionately convicted that something in reality, usually about other people is the case even though it's not true. B. We are believing beyond the refutation of what others believe that this is the case, even when it is not the case. C. We are incapable of being corrected by other about this same false belief. "Karl Jaspers set out to alert psychiatry at large to the principal criteria for delusion –absolute conviction; incorrigibility; and impossibility of content." (Gorski, M., 2012, pp. 1)   Second, Jasper also says that while we are having a delusion we are brought up into a state of confusion he calls a "delusional cloud" or "delusional mood." In this confused state of mind we could be said to have a subjective passion to believe something that is just not true. "Delusional mood, classically defined in his writings, involves an enigmatic transformation distinct from typical states of dysphoria or anxiety." (Sass, L., Byron, G., 2015, pp. 298) Third, delusion is ultimately rationally un-understandable. "In this section my object has been to introduce the primary experience of delusion as one of the true criteria of pathologically falsified judgement: and un-understandability as its trade – or hallmark of a proprium (the primary experience of delusion proper), and propria and accidents are logically- and of course, metaphysically-distinct." (Gorski, M. 2012, pp. 6) Fourth, an important concept here is delusion is based on a primary experience, according to Jasper. A primary experience is the one that has apparently came alive in our head, and not one derived from other secondary emotions that could follow. "The primary traceable to the illness is that experience that cannot be understood or psychologically derived from other experiences." (Giovanni, Stanghelliini, 2012, pp.2) (If we really want to perceive a particular object of fascination in the light of a primary experience, then it follows that it would not be in order to add in any other thoughts like a symbolic meaning coming alive then too, to it to be listed as part of the same experience.)

Conrad

Next we have Klaus Conrad come along in the 1950's with a modified understanding about the nature of delusion that we need be aware of. For Conrad delusion is rationally understandable. For Conrad delusion is really a symbolic meaning coming alive to what one witnesses or thinks that then makes this same person to believe that they are being sent a message by others when it is not the case. This is the crucial difference between Jasper and Conrad, as Jasper instead thought delusion was not rationally understandable at all. This represents a big change in how we possibly understand delusion. If we can know what the exact thought that this person was having that triggered a reaction that turns into a false belief, then this should give us the key to understanding the true nature of this same delusion that one can now be more likely to overcome. If we are to compare the overall understanding of delusion according to Conrad in contrast to Jasper: (1) Like Jasper, Conrad thought it to be the case that delusion involves conviction, incorrigibility, and irrefutability (as he does not challenge the definition of delusion but insists on subjective passion in effect like Jasper) (2) Like Jasper, Conrad also believes in the delusional cloud- a cloud of subjective passion that represents a confused state), but modifies the understanding of it somewhat. For Conrad the experience in the delusional cloud is changed with a new experience within it that Conrad calls the "aha" experience. In the aha experience he or she entering delusion may decide on a particular potential symbolic meaning coming alive to what they saw that they now think is a secret message sent by others. "The transition from delusional mood to the Aha-Erlebnes of the delusional revelation occurs precisely at the moment of loss of the patient's ability to distance from the experience, ie, "to achieve an exchange of reference frames, or perspectives, even if only temporarily- with the eyes of the other(s)." (Mishara, A., L., 2009, pp.3) (3) Unlike Jasper though Conrad believes that delusion is ultimately rationally understandable in the form of this new found "symbolism" that the patient thinks may really be a message from others when it is not the case. "Borrowing from ancient Greek, the artificial term apophany describes this process of repetitively and monotonously experiencing abnormal meanings in the entire surrounding experimental field, eg, being observed, spoken about, the object of eavesdropping followed by strangers.") (Mishara, A., L., 2009, pp.3) (4) For Conrad then delusion is a secondary delusion as opposed to a primary delusion because it involves the transition from literally just witnessing or hearing something to then freezing on a particular referential frame of experience where symbolism now comes alive with emotion to the person entering delusion. "The patient often interprets the course of events as if a film were being made or a theatre-piece performed."). (Mishara, A., L., 2009, pp.3)

Two Contemporary Researchers on Delusion

Murakami

Murakami like Conrad and yet other contemporary schizophrenic researchers believe together that delusion is not altogether an un-understandable enterprise. Murakami like Conrad thinks that there is symbolic meaning coming alive to what one sees that explains why the person entering delusion could override the superior evidence that suggests otherwise, which you should ordinarily heed. In Affection Of Contact And Transcendental Telepathy In Schizophrenia And Autism, Murakami offers a story about two children with autism that are playing with a stone like it is really a cake. As part of this experience they apparently actually begin to think that the stone is really literally a cake. Murakami calls this belief on the subjective will of these autistic children to honestly believe that this stone is literally really a piece of cake means they are entering a "Phantasia" The concept of "Phantasia" means something similar to Jasper's "delusion cloud" in that it too implies a "confused state of mind." The concept of "Phantasia" itself means "the "imagination without clear image" the "imagination without intentional object" (Murakami, Y., 2013, pp. 2). Murakami uses the expression "double meanings" to describe how one could see one thing but yet see it with a new meaning at the same time. "In perceiving and handling the stones, a child sees them as "cake", and he (she) simulates the "eating." (Murakami, Y., 2013, pp.3) In the case of those with autism though- at least sometimes they apparently mista30ke a metaphor itself then for what it literally represents. Murakami uses a real example of this by them to illustrate how this is the case sometimes. So now the use of symbolism is apparently real to all of us, but that we are not all tricked into mistaking the metaphorical for the literal when the two are substituted for purposes of making a figurative comparison between the two.

For those with "schizophrenia" they think that they are really being sent a "message" using "metaphors and symbolic meaning" to do so. For Murakami a schizophrenic also experiences a phantasia or confused state of mind while entering delusion wherein they are experiencing a "terrifying other" coming alive to what they are experiencing. "In contrast, the terrifying other in the schizophrenic hallucination has an acute otherness." (Murakami, Y., 2013, pp. 8) (The otherness that is terrifying them eventually turns into who they might think could be trying then to send them a message.) For Murakami the schizophrenic is incapable of "transcendental telepathy where one can rise with communication above an internal dilemma about a double meaning to what one sees that also includes a necessary otherness to account for it. The schizophrenic experiences what he calls pathological telepathy instead transmitted by unknown others. "It replaces transcendental telepathy with pathological telepathy. The perceptual phantasia is no longer a thought communicated by the interlocker, but all perceptual objects have a double meaning (so to speak a "pathological" perceptual phantasia) is transmitted by unknown others." (Murakami, Y., 2013, PP. 9) The schizophrenic just like the autistic person sometimes stays confused about the real meaning of what turns out to be just a metaphorical comparison in a little bit different way than those with autism apparently sometimes do in another way. Once again the autistic person at a very young age anyways is swayed by an imagination that changes the use of a metaphorical comparison into believing that which the metaphor to them literally implies. The schizophrenic believes that the use a of a metaphor or symbolic meaning coming alive means a terrifying other which could turn out to be a message being sent by others, when this is not the case and not to be believed, but instead the whole thing really may be just a coincidence.

Pickard

For Pickard, another modern contemporary researcher, she offers in The Epistemology of The Self, an example of someone that is having a delusion wherein they think that they are being sent messages by an alien force. The alien force is attempting to use the scenery that they are being exposed to, to leave hints with a particular meaning, or then message to it. "In the first of these patient reports, the conscious, occurent mental event that is experienced as alien is an impulse- indeed, an impulse to perform a wrongful and arguably aggressive act." (Pickard, H., 2010, pp.57) "Standard examples of patent reports attribute the alien mental event to another person or group of people" (Pickard, H., 2010, pp. 57). This kind of fanciful imagination is when one attributes to an alien force a message sent to them when this is just not the case. "Alien thought is a first-rank, diagnostically central symptom of schizophrenia. It is attributed when schizophrenics report that they have conscious mental events that are not their own" (Pickard, H., 2010, pp.55). (This to me implies to me a state of mind related to how they came up with their "fearful thought" that first involves a "confusion" about whether they or somebody else controls their very thought process. This in one sense then reminds me

of the "delusional cloud" by Jasper or even "Phantasia according to Murakami, but not

quite as complex and potentially complicated to understand as either one of these.

Pickard's alien force simply does not completely "tie up" the analysis of how one enters

delusion like Jasper's "delusional cloud" or even Murakami's "Phantasia" seems to.

It is interesting to me that that upon examination of the steps in the thought

process during the entrance of delusion that even Pickard seems to get to the point more

in terms of understanding the entrance of delusion than what once went on in our

understanding of it. Although she still bothers to allude to Frith's ambiguous Cognitive

model of thought to better understand the nature of delusion, it is clear to me that overall

there is a desire in her and other modern researchers to try to get to the point more now in

terms of how we understand this disorder. Instead of just glossing over how one may be

said to have intense fear during the entrance of delusion, let' not stop there in the analysis

of it, but move along to see the whole experience in on quick glance! Look the actual

account of the person that believed that an alien force was haunting them was stated

straight out in the article, which got me to realize that in just four simple steps of the

thought process itself one could be said to be entering delusion! First, this person

literally witnessed in the same environment what becomes the object of their fascination.

Second, they see a symbolic meaning coming alive that symbolizes something beyond

what one can literally see, where they are wondering whether someone is controlling their

thought process itself. Third, this same person thinks that an alien force must be sending them messages because of the kind of symbolism that has come alive to them. Fourth, they now believe for sure that an alien force is both controlling their thoughts and sending them messages too. To think about the entrance of delusion itself in just four simple steps really tells the truth and gets to the point like we should on our understanding of delusion. This is what we need to know to better help solve what might be said to cause delusion and not getting lost in some ridiculous witch hunt that overcomplicates what is actually going on in the thought process during the entrance of delusion. What's wrong with getting to the point instead of just go on and on like Jasper or others before Conrad that highlighted a more complicated understanding of delusion? It is obvious to me that what we need to better understand the entrance of delusion that can be by now understood in just four simple steps if the truth is revealed! The following is a diagram that I myself composed that attempts to give a plausible understanding of this process!

My Diagram

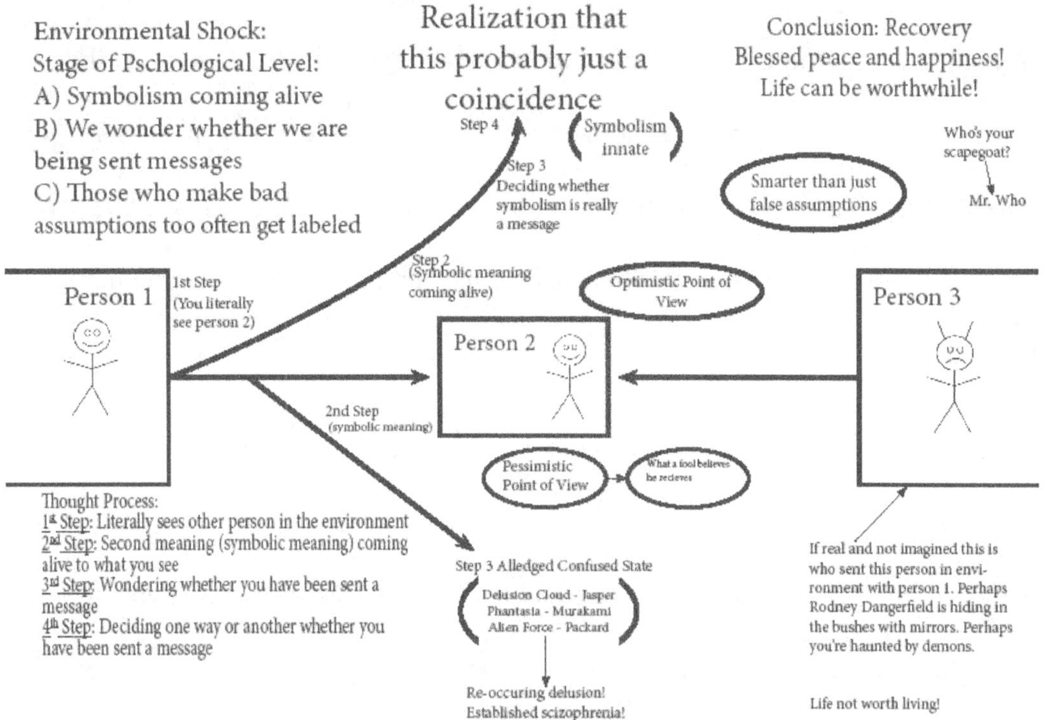

To show how someone could be said to enter delusion I have made up the above diagram highlighting what I believe to be a plausible likely illustration of the thought process itself that goes on during the entrance of it. This diagram consists of just four basic, simple steps that one could be said to experience during the entrance of delusion which I believe gives a direct, honest, revealing, but to the point analysis of the thought process itself as delusion or hallucination takes over: Step 1: the person literally witness whatever in the environment-most of the time the behavior or at least presence of another person that captures their attention. Step 2: They see a symbolic or double meaning coming alive in regards to this same object of perception. Step 3: They wonder whether they are being sent a message from another or others by way of the symbolic meaning that comes alive in their mind: (was the symbolic meaning coming alive to what they literally witnessed a message being sent them from someone else or just an innate coincidence? Step 4: Finally you either choose to believe or disbelieve that others are trying to send you a message by way of what you may actually have witnessed that captivated your attention initially.

My diagram is to be perceived as an objective tool to put in perspective the thought process itself that goes on during the entrance of delusion. This diagram is not an attempt to reinforce that delusion always happens in exactly four major steps universally, (as fluctuation in the number of steps in the thought process could happen), but it is still useful for "revealing" how one's thoughts lead one to the next in a simple basic logical progression that can be plotted.   Then I would like to stress too that with the right coaching one might rise above delusion. This involves learning to ignore a "false conviction" about "whatever issue" in question, when it is the case that there is superior evidence to the contrary.

The Fiction Story

Next let me present you with a fictitious story of my own about how one could succumb to delusion, but with the right education about delusion- using this same diagram of mine which reveals what turns out to be an overall flaw in the thought process of this person while entering delusion. We can then pinpoint where this person went astray and how they might turn the whole thing around for the better.

Suppose that you were just hired a few days earlier in a new factory job. On one particular day in question after only a few weeks of working there you happen to have a real bad day at work. On this particular day you were moved to a different job where the work was faster pace and more difficult for you. Halfway thru the day you after just a short time on this new job you are just sure that it is really not for you. You are told that you are stuck with this new job for at least a few days so you had better make the best of it. Even in the afternoon when you attempted to baton down the hatches so to speak on this new job it was painstaking just to get thru it. Whereas you started out loving your job that you had, this morning things were now getting out of hand negatively. You really feel like quitting, and instead of anyone trying to jump up and tell that you would be missed not one co-worker says anything that is supportive of you just hanging in there for more. Then at almost 5:00 pm though when it was quitting time you found yourself face to face with the supervisor. He congratulates you on your ability to hang in there when the going gets tough and says too that he looks forward to hiring you soon if you can keep up the good work. This of course you appreciated immensely!

But now just moments later when you were standing in line to punch at the end of the shift, while looking straight ahead, you notice a big guy that you think you don't like smile right at you. You think that this is really a smile of sarcasm to get you to be intimidated and scared, so you will just give up and forget about working there. Why he was never friendly to you –in fact you at least seen him at a distance one time talking to a co-worker- you think portraying you in a negative light. You think too that his smile represents the possibility that tomorrow him and some of his friends might attempt to discourage you further one way or another about winning employment there. You think that all you need is just one more bad day, even after receiving moral support from the supervisor and you just might be discouraged enough to just give up. Anyways you resent this guy smiling at you because once again you perceive his motive in a negative light, and "yes" just maybe there is really some "up and coming" kind of conspiracy against you continuing to work there by this big guy and his friends.

Trauma

Now just for a moment let's think about the nature of delusion in general in light of the steps of the thought process that is going on when one enters delusion and ask ourselves how things went wrong to the point that this disorder would set in? It is really in the second step of the thought process entering delusion that one now visualizes in their mind a potential symbolic meaning coming alive to what they just literally witnessed in the first step. It is right here where this same person becomes perplexed about the meaning of the symbolism that comes alive to them, that they literally saw, heard, or just thought about. Instead of the symbolic meaning that is coming alive to them just being perceived as a coincidence, it is possible to believe that this symbolism that one attaches to what they literally saw as being more than that……! It is possible that right here "wonderment" or even "confusion" sets in as to the significance of what this symbolism could be said to possibly imply- like is someone attempting to send them a message?

Next, asking this question itself about the significance of the symbolic meaning coming alive to you constitutes the third step in the thought process itself in entering delusion where you may be on your way to believing a lie. By the fourth step in this same thought process this person is now sometimes believing that they are being sent a message by others, when in the light of what they rationally know it is not to be believed. Well what serves as an explanation of why someone that may be ordinarily a reflective and intelligent person now believe something ridiculous, when superior evidence should get you to believe otherwise?

We are told by experts that "trauma" from our childhood plays an important role in making one fearful, or aversive because of a bad experience growing up with others. We are told that there may be a particular memory or memories locked in their sub-conscious that cause them to fear, doubt, or to avoid others. Their overall ability to trust others is sometimes lessened. Friendship relationships to may be thwarted as a result. Trauma that one experienced somewhere earlier on in life may really affect our ability adversely to not think positively enough just in everyday circumstances where this can prevent us from interacting as positively as we should with others, including establishing healthy interactions with others like we should. In (Ingo Schafer and Helen Fisher Childhood Trauma & Psychosis-What Is the Evidence)

The evidence for an association between childhood trauma and psychosis is steadily accumulating, and exploration of potential mechanistic pathways has begun. Emerging findings from longitudinal studies and demonstration of a dose-response relationship in others suggest a role of childhood trauma in the development of psychosis. The relative influence of other variables in this relationship, however, warrants further investigation. Independent from the question of causality, childhood trauma and PTSD are frequent in patients with psychosis and severely affect, course and outcome. More research is therefore needed to further develop and evaluate appropriate treatments for psychotic patients suffering from the consequences of childhood trauma. Nevertheless, the existing trials suggest that patients with psychotic disorders can benefit from both present-focused and trauma-focused treatments, despite severe symptoms, suicidal thinking, and vulnerability to hospitalizations.

Then too there is the stress and even potential trauma to what goes on right now with what you are presently experiencing - (which I have already mentioned in the list of potential causes of schizophrenia.).

Related to our present environment, or our social arrangement that we are under, or the psychological changes in general that we go through may directly affect our ability to work and get along with others effectively in everyday life- the psychological changes that we endure under stress growing into a fully competent adult from teen years can be almost overwhelming at times getting there.

It is of course possible to receive counseling from a professional for childhood trauma or the stress and shock that you are presently experiencing either one, but there is no real guarantee that this in itself or all by itself will actually get rid of your unwarranted fears and reactions of mistrust, withdrawal, or uncalled for anger, especially when it borderlines with delusion.

So now what can we do to overcome falling into the same trap of delusion besides get therapy itself for trauma, stress and shock that we may have experienced? Well what might a more positive attitude in general accomplish for us even if we have been hurt psychologically as a child or in our life since then? No doubt healthy interactions with others and an overall positive attitude towards others helps us get along better with them and accomplish more on the job or in life in general. Just to maintain a positive attitude in life towards others can be invaluable whether we are fully enlightened or not. Reconstructing a stronger self, even after trauma and stress, is possible.

The Fonz?

For example let's just for a second remember a 1970's sitcom called "Happy Days" wherein Henry Winkler starred as the "Fonz" He is a kool motor cycler that for a young person has "little delusion" and cares not only just for himself but likes his friends too. He is "hell bent" on leading them into a positive adventure, with a positive plan to show everyone how to get along, change the world for the better where liking each other is no object! The "Fonz" is the young people's icon! The Fonz can really "walk on the water" so to speak with how he "wheels and deals" in everyday life! Virtually everyone I know that has watched many "Happy Days" episodes is a big fan of Henry Winkler the Fonz! People brag on the Fonz for being a fun innovative character that even serves as a mentor for the young people!

Or Cat in The Hat?

Then too there was in the 1960's the creation of an animated cartoon character by Dr. Zuess called none other than "Cat In the Hat." The character Cat in The Hat was used for short stories that was about a cat that was somewhat self-centered and also arrogant that just couldn't find the handle on how to do things properly, where he indeed made a mess out of literally everything that he did. He does not seem to understand cause and effect in terms of what works just to be able to function competently, accordingly. He is an unruly, individualistic character that apparently does not "know himself" or "understand himself" even after the wisdom of William Shakespeare the great playwright and other great thinkers affirmed that we should know and understand ourselves. The character "Cat In The Hat" is a loveable character just the same, but as you follow his actions in the story your compassion for him may turn into pity, but then even disgust if you stop and think about it for too long. Although "Cat In the Hat" can be funny, he is too stupid to take seriously. If we are to compare the character the Fonz with Cat in the Hat, both of them are lovable and amusing up to a point, but we see that the Fonz is one that you revere and look up to, while Cat in the Hat is way too often idiotic, a klutz and even grief causer, to revere being. Do you know anybody who wants to be perceived as a goofy klutz like "Cat in the hat" or would we all like to be somebody that is staying on top of things properly and has plenty of friends too like the Fonz. The Fonz is better organized and self-adjusted for interaction with others than Cat In The Hat who is obviously a disorganized mess. Cat in the Hat lacks communication skills, but plunders on with mistakes like in the Beatle's "Nowhere Man" song. When things go wrong instead of develop fuller communication skills for guidance from others, Cat In the Hat is someone that is all the time making mistakes and possibly even could be said to probably be full of "delusion" based on his behavior. He is not in reality because he has apparently not learned to be fully rational like one should be. Instead he lives in a world of potential fear, doubt, and confusion. Synthesized interactions with others that is helpful in this regard is in order. Getting along with others in everyday life is essential for complete success sometimes. "Delusion" hurts and destroys, but an attitude of friendship and co-operation by us will bring more potential opportunity for us all. If we can just perceive ourselves in a positive enough light in how we deal with others, that includes something more than just a vain selfish image, but also aware of a real world full of others that need real love this should help us succeed in the long- run. A good attitude overcomes delusion better, and helps one stand their ground better in the face of adversity.

Adjusting Your Thinking to Reality

Now let's plug into this diagram one more time this same story continued with a different ending then what I just described. Suppose that this same young man that thinks he is not welcome where he works-even though it's not true- and realized in his head that this is probably ridiculous that anybody is out to really take away his job there. He then immediately becomes more confident and more than that he wins the opportunity for permanent employment where he is at. Also instead of going on in animosity and suspicion of the big guy that was ahead of him they finally make friends. This young new employee is beginning to feel as kool as the Fonz himself at work and not some simple confused person that lacks enough confidence. So let's first re-trace the first step where the big guy in front of him at the time clock smiled at him. This time when he reruns this same incident thru his head he does not get paranoid and believe that which is not true about the real meaning of the behavior of others- or another in this case. In the first step he does see this same guy turn around and smile at him at the time clock. In the second step he does indeed consider a full range of potential meaning to what this could possibly imply.   In the third step when he is deciding whether to believe or not for sure whether he was actually being sent a negative message he is not swayed by unnatural fear over what common sense would tell you- that there is no sinister plan. In the fourth step he decides not to believe that this guy really was trying to send him a negative message of ill-will. In this scenario just mentioned this same new guy on the job resists and rises above all delusion that he could otherwise be experiencing! He is now turning into a winner. He is making friends within a broad range of people including making friends with whom he thought despised and hated him. Without delusion in his life he is doing so much better than he would have. He has friends more than he did, and he is adding up his life much more quickly than he would with delusion in it. To stop and take everything personal when we shouldn't is a loser!

What resembles delusion?

Finally, there are yet "other reasons" too why someone might mistakenly misconstrue the real meaning and intent of other people's behavior let's say other than delusion. Let me give you three other ways in which one can be said to make false judgements about others that are in actuality really not technically delusion, but are like it:

First it is possible to make "assumptions" in everyday life that we shouldn't that may bring us to the same false conclusion that a delusion could also do, but is still not the same as delusion. An "assumption" is "something taken for granted or accepted as true without proof, a supposition; (Free Dictionary), whereas a delusion is based on a "false conviction" by itself that is dubious in terms of its believability in light of good common sense. How many times have we all-in fact, raced to a false conclusion about "whatever" that misconstrued in some way the true meaning and intent of others

behavior? It is obviously quite a common experience that someone being careless that

did not bother to know the facts about whatever and then because of the assumption made

also jump to a false conclusion about the true meaning of the behavior of others or

whatever else is the issue. And yes this indeed can and does have negative consequences

for all of us when this happens. And one of these negative consequences could even be

to get labeled a schizophrenic or delusional person, when in reality you were just making

assumptions that you shouldn't.

Second it is possible to have a problem with your "memory" that is known as

confabulation. Confabulation is the "unconscious filling in of gaps in memory with

fabricated facts and experiences, commonly associated with organic pathology. It differs

from lying in that the patient has no intention to deceive and believes the fabricated

memories to be real" (Free Dictionary). Now to experience confabulation might get one

to be labeled delusional of a kind in a way that is really "bizarre" and "un-

understandable", when in reality the "faulty reasoning" itself is related to a memory loss

that has caused one to believe false information that could be said to include the meaning

of the behavior of other people when this is the issue.

Third, you could get mislabeled delusional and then schizophrenic based on

behavior that exhibits the quality of "attribution". Attribution is "an inference about the

cause of a particular person's behavior(s) or of an observed action or event" (Free

Dictionary). In effect attribution is blaming others for what we ourselves are responsible for. . This of course can sometimes be perceived as a "plain ole lie" someone tells you about the other guy for convenience sake let's say and not based on a true "conviction" of someone which of course a necessary in order for it or to qualify for being a delusion.

(Something else to keep in mind is that as it pertains to this diagram itself, it can be used for any and all kinds of delusion or even hallucinations with only little modification to it. The first step might be used for an incident describing hallucination, where someone just imagined in their head that they saw someone appear in front of them, where this was just a fantasy.   The other three steps too can be modified accordingly with any kind of delusion or hallucination.)

(Next, a word of caution to anyone like myself that is an optimist about one's ability to overcome delusion. Delusion is usually attached to serious psychosis where it may not be always quite as quick and automatic to overcome delusion as easily as we might want it to be. A responsible person on this issue should be willing to realize that it sometimes takes time to bring people out of delusion so we should not get impatient and pushy with the patient about doing this necessarily at the snap of one's fingers. We should not try to intimidate the patient of delusion and schizophrenia in any way, but encourage them to be positive and do their best, hoping for recovery for them. Delusion is "real" and "potentially dangerous", even though with the right help it can sometimes be overcome. This may include trained professional help in psychiatry to assist them in

their recovery.)

Part IV Treatment

The History of Treatment for Schizophrenia

Once upon a time before WWII, most people that were considered to have a

serious mental illness were shut away in mental hospitals for the rest of their life. "For

more than half of the twentieth century, most people diagnosed with serious

schizophrenia were institutionalized in a public mental hospital." (Ronald Comer, 2007,

pp.495)

After WWII many of the soldiers that served in WWII came back brain shocked from the war and needed counseling. The rise of outpatient counseling began to develop out- patient facilities then that began to grow rapidly, where one could get the medical help that they need for their sickness. The general population too got in on the new kind of out-patient medical treatment that was becoming more and more popular. Outpatient doctors and psychiatrists were now treating the general population at out-patient clinics from everything from depression right up thru schizophrenia. Outpatient treatment for those with mental illness proved very quickly quite successful. Even those that were psychotic with schizophrenia that ordinarily might be hospitalized for long periods of time were now allowed to stay in the free world-many of them not only taking care of themselves, but working jobs on their own, being productive citizens. According to Ronal Comer:

In the 1950's, clinicians developed two institutional approaches that finally brought some hope to patients who and lived in institutions for years: milieu therapy, based on humanistic principles and the token economy program based on behavioral principles. These approached particularly helped improve the personal care and self-image of patient's problem areas that had been worsened by institutionalization. The approaches were soon adapted by many institutions and are now standard features of institutional care.)

Sometimes still though in the case of serious mental illness people still need hospitalization- at least from time to time, but were not coerced into stay there for necessarily any great length of time. In Recovery From Delusions, which was a study about those temporarily hospitalized for delusion, the patients being tested recovered from there delusional state within less than a month's time. It usually took about twenty days on the average for them to come back out of a delusional state with the help of anti-psychotic drugs and therapy at the hospital.

According to this same article there are three general phases in coming back out of delusion. "Based on these findings, we have defined three stages in the course of delusional thinking. Initially, in the delusional phase, the patient is totally involved in his delusions. This is followed by the double-awareness phase, where reality testing and trust coexist with the delusions. On recovery, a third, non-delusional phase occurs." (Sacks, M., H., Carpenter, W., T., Strauss, J., S., Bethesda, 1974, pg. 118) It is important to know though that there is no guarantee that they will not be plagued again by a new delusion, but for the time being when they show significant signs of recovery from delusion they are then allowed to stay in the free world once again. Now of course we want long-term recovery from delusion and not just short-term relief from it, but there is no absolute guarantee that the patient will not fall into delusion again.-especially without continued therapy of medicine and counseling.

Today's Treatment

Antipsychotic drugs

Antipsychotic drugs for the patient with schizophrenia are important if a full recovery is going to happen. "A cross sectional survey was administered to 250 patients with a primary clinical diagnosis of a as schizophrenia spectrum disorder across five outpatient clinics in the United States….a total of 87.6% of respondents identified the ability to think more clearly as an important property of the medication." (Archtypes, E., Simmons, A., Skabeev, A., Levy, N., Jiang, Y., Marc, P., 2018, pp.17) This of course is very strong testimony of support by the patient themselves in favor of the continued use of anti-psychotic drugs to fight their illness. This serves to help make the overall continued analysis that anti-psychotic drugs do indeed have positive benefits for the patient of schizophrenia or bipolar.

Therapy

A. Education

Next, the patients of today with schizophrenia are being taught Self-management education for them. Although self-management education programs for persons with schizophrenia are being developed and advocated, uncertainty about their overall effectiveness remains.   The effectiveness of education on the nature of the disorder itself is still in its development and the long-run outcome of this has not been demonstrated yet. "Although, self-management education programs for persons with schizophrenia that include education on the nature of this disorder itself is being developed and advocated, uncertainty about their effectiveness remains……. Finally 13 studies with 1404 people were included. Self-management education interventions were associated with a significant reduction of relapse events and re-hospitalization." Zou, H., Zheng L., Nolan, M., Arthur, D., Wang H., Hu, L., 2013, pp.256)

It is not difficult for just anyone to realize that to be better educated about a disorder, that you could be said to be suffering from, could possibly help alleviate the symptoms of the disorder. Since the 1950's and 1960's most of the people that are said to have schizophrenia or bi-polar now remain in the free world when they are willing to participate in outpatient therapy, take the antipsychotic drugs on a regular basis that has been prescribed for them and at least get along with others in everyday life in a satisfactory enough way then they usually win the chance to stay in the free world. But now with more personal education on the nature of the disorder itself as part of the therapy this should help increase the number of people that rise above the major symptoms of this disorder altogether in time as a result.

B. Attitude

An overall good attitude in general on the part of the patient is important for recovery. In a quite useful journal article by Paul Lysaker, Jack Tsai, Kristin Hammond & Louanne W. Davis Called Patterns of coping Preference Among Persons With Schizophrenia: A study was made involving 133 people.

In particular we were interested in whether we could detect five different

groups of persons based on preferences for four preferences for four types of coping

in to five groups according to coping preference of the particular individuals in this

study based on four types of coping i) "Persons who had a preference for both acting

and considering, ii) persons who had a preference for acting alone, iii) persons who

had a preference for considering and resigning; iv) persons with a preference for

ignoring and persons with v) no clear preference for any coping style.

Of the five different groups that were put together the Acting and Considering

group did the best. As predicted, the Acting and Considering group when compared to the

other groups tended to have greater levels of function on both self-report instruments and

objective ratings. They had higher levels of hope, self-esteem and less emotional

discomfort than all other groups. They had significantly more of the foundations

necessary for interpersonal relationships than No Preference or Resigning group. There

was no evidence that the Acting and Considering group had lesser levels of positive

symptoms, negative or general symptoms of anxiety. Importantly, there was no evidence

that this or other groups tended to distort their responses in a manner to defensively

enhance their self-image. (Lsysaker, Tsai, Hammond, and Davis, pp. 198)

So now to be considerate to others and be action oriented in general more helps to

get people to think better where they now work together better with others. So here is proof that among schizophrenics a positive attitude does play an important role in helping us to succeed in everyday life to get along with others better.

Finally, on the topic of a positive attitude on the part of the patient let me next mention a couple of self-help programs in particular that are available to anyone who needs them among the masses that make numerous claims that for just anyone they will help enhance a more positive attitude in general towards others: 1) Exercise 2) Transcendental Meditation

First, all over the country health spas have sprung up to help get people back into tip- top physical and mental health. Millions of books on exercising have been written and are being sold to others as well. If one takes better care of his or her physical health they also will can almost always be said to be taking better care of their psychological health. It is a proven fact that exercise is not only good for your body, but you mind as well. As it pertains to physical exercise for those with schizophrenia in particular it has been demonstrated that it has positive effects for them, and it is highly recommended, but a schizophrenic in general is less likely to work out with physical exercise than others. "There is clear evidence that proves the physical and psychological health benefits of physical activity (PA) in patients with schizophrenia (Dauwan, Bergemann, Heringa, & Sommer, 2016; Gorczynski & Faulkner, 2010). However, patients with schizophrenia are more likely to be less physical active than the general population (Faulkner, Cohn, & Remington, 2006 LIndamer et al, 2008; Stubbs et al, 2005). (Faulkner, Cohn, &

Remington, 2006;" (Costa, R., Bastos, T., Pobst, M., Seabra, A., Vihena, E., and Corredeira, R., (2018) It even helps to give us all out-loud encouragement to exercise since this is good for our health.

Second, the need to give your nervous system deep rest may come along the way in life even as young person especially can become extremely helpful. Sometimes linked to stress young people begin to slip from reality- perhaps crushed inside by what is presently going on in their life right now. Transcendental Meditation is a viable means to give your nervous system the deep rest that it needs. There is literally tons of factual evidence to support that TM when practiced correctly brings about physiological and psychological change both in someone for the better. First, to put forward- reduced drug abuse alcohol use. "A retrospective study of 1,862 subjects who practiced the Transcendental Meditation technique an average of 20 months showed decreased in the reported us of non-prescribed drugs." (Denniston, D., McWilliams, P., 1975) Another claim by the proponents of Transcendental Meditation is that increased self –actualization occurs as a result. "Growth of self-actualization as defined by this test includes the development of the following qualities: open, receptive, caring attitude, cheerfulness and good humor; predominance of positive thinking; spontaneity and freshness of appreciation; self-sufficiency ; loss of fear of death; affective readiness for developing consciousness; discovery of opportunities for creativity; acceptance of self, nature, and others; conscious sense of destiny." (Denniston, D., McWilliams, P., 1975) There is no guarantee of course that even if one does TM that this will necessarily solve all of your problems including that of delusion, but it should enhance your ability to do things more effectively that are constructive and helpful towards others if that's what you choose to do. TM should also be seen as a vehicle that pushes people to a more enlightened self.

Part V Education for us All!

Not only is education on the nature of this disorder being used to help treat the patient by a psychiatric doctor or counselor, but are also taught at colleges or universities, and there are many, many new books by credible researchers on schizophrenia that are being sold to the general public that should continue to wake up the masses about the nature of this disorder. It too is my goal with my master's thesis to make everyone literate on schizophrenia and interrelated disorders, so that one can much more easily rise above schizophrenic symptoms. I can very vividly remember how it was the case that I did not have parents that were professionals in law or business when I was a kid and it definitely made the first three years of my college life tougher simply because I did not have a clear, full, concrete understanding of the related vocabulary and concepts to acquire a much fuller understanding of human relationships in law and money. When I finally began to learn and understand the concepts that were in these fields it woke me up about a lot of things. Now after all of these years I want to help make the next generation more literate and educated in general about schizophrenia. I'm convinced that to educate the masses on what schizophrenia entails to should clear up a lot of confusion and help to prevent more delusional thinking.

As it pertains to the discussion of delusion that I made in Part III, I first gave a brief discussion of the history of ideas that pertain to the people that pioneered this concept, and then ended it with a discussion of how one might more easily rise above it with a more rational understanding of its mechanics itself: (For someone that is about to enter delusion, (1) This same person literally witnessed, heard, or thought about whatever object of fascination. (2) They then experience a symbolic meaning coming alive to it. (3) They wonder whether they are being sent a message. (4) They decide in their head whether they are being sent a message. We really don't all jump to false conclusions about others we imagine a sinister plan to us by others just because of absurd distorted leaps of judgement about the meaning of the behavior of others. Most people are smart enough to realize that people in motion let's say for instance that are just doing their own thing really has nothing to do with them personally. But what about those that still fall victim to delusion? Well let's get them smart enough to rise above delusion too. Let's

by all means keep educating everyone about the nature of delusion, so that the next

generation will not be duped into delusion about others.

A positive attitude in general life towards others we should all have as it should

enhance our ability to get along better with them. People that are more positive in how

they treat others, tend to have more loving relationships too, whereas hate, contempt, and

indifference for one another goes nowhere. Delusion itself should now be easier to

overcome if we learn to like and accept others, realizing that they too are just in situation

trying to survive that we can even become friends with sometimes then this should

eliminate uncalled for suspicion and potential animosity towards others.   And as they

say, "the world is as we are!" And as they say, "a good attitude is everything!"

Bibliography

American Psychiatric Association (2013) Diagnostic Statistical Manual, American

Psychiatric Publishing, 5th Ed. Vol 7 pp. 104

Archtypes, E., Simmons, A., Skabeev, A., Levy, N., Jiang, Y., Marc, P., (2018) Patient

Preferences

Concerning the efficacy and Side Effect Profile of Schizophrenic medications: a Survey

of Patients Living With Schizophrenia, BMC Psychiatry, 18;292, pp..1 DOI

10.1186/s12888-018.1856.y

Assumption. (nd) in the Free dictionary retrieved from Free Dictionary. the free

dictionary.com/assumtion Attribution. (nd) in the Free dictionary retrieved from

Medical dictionary. the free dictionary. com/attribution

Comer, RJ (2007)Abnormal Psychology ninth Ed., New York : Worth Publishers pp.495

Confabulation. (nd) The Free Dictionary retrieved from Medical Dictionary. the

free dictionary.com/confabulation

Costa, R., Bastos, T., Probst, M., Seabra, A., Vilhena, E., and Corredeira, R., (2018)

Autonomous Motivation And Quality Of Life As predictors Of physical Activity

In Patients With Schizophrenia International Journal of Psychiatry in Clinical

Practice 22:3, pp. 184-190 DOI 10. 108013651501.2018.1435821)

Counter, P, Spillane, R. (2017) On The Legacy Of Thomas Szasz: A Reiteration Of The

Myth Of Mental Illness and Recent Criticism. Ethical Human Psychology and

Psychiatry, 19, (3)   pp.151

Denniston, D., McWilliams, P., (1975) The TM Book, Allen Park, Michigan:

Three Rivers Press, pp. 203

Fallon, L.F. (2013), Schizohrenia. , In Gale (Ed.) The Gale Encyclopedia Of Nursing and

Allied Health, schizophrenia pp. 2

Giovanni, Stanghellini, (2012), Jaspers On "Primary" Delusions, John Hopkins

University Press, 19, (2), pp. 87-89,154

Goffman, E., (1959), The Presentation of the Self In Everyday Life, New York: Anchor

Books

Gordski, M., (2012), Karl Jaspers On Delusion Definition Genus and Specific Difference,

19, (2) pp.1-9

Johnson, P., (2015) About Delusion-Diagram

Leong, F. T. L. , Kalibatseva, Z. (2011) Cross-Cultural Barriers To Mental Health

Services In The United States, Cerebrum The Dana forum on Brain

Science,2011,5 pp. (1-6)

Lysaker, P., Tsai, J., Davis, H & L., Patterns of Coping Preference Among Persons With

Schizophrenia; Associations With Self-Esteem, Hope, Symptoms And Function,

International Journal Of Behavioral Consultation And Therapy, 5, (2), pp. 198

Mishara, A.L., (2010), Klaus Conrad (1905-1961): Delusion Mood, Psychosis, and

Beginning

Schizophrenia, Schizophrenia Bulletin 36, (1) DOI: 10.1093/schbulsbp144

Murakami, Y.(2013), Affection Of Contact And Transcendental Telepathy In

Schizophrenia and Autism, Springer Link, 12,(1), pp. 179-194 Paranoia. (nd) in

Free Dictionary retrieved from The Free Dictionary.com/paranoia Paranoid

ideation. (nd) in Psychology Dictionary retrieved from the Psychology

Dictionary.35

Pickard, H., (2010), Schizophrenia And The Epistemology Of Self-Knowledge,

University of Oxford, 6, (1), pp. 55-7345.

Ruiz, D., (1960) Epidemiology Of Schizophrenia; Some Diagnostic Sociocultural

Considerations, Phylon 43(4), pp. 315-326 DOI: 10.2307/2754

Saavedra, J. Lopez M., Gonzales, S., Cubero, R. (2016), Does Employment Promote

Recovery? Meanings From Work Experience In People Diagnosed With Serious

Mental Illness, Cult Med Psychiatry, pp.. 511 DOI 10.1007/s 11013-015-9481-4

Sacks, M., H., Carpenter, W., T., Strauss, J., S., Bethesda, 1974, Recovery from

Delusions, arch Gen Arch.Gen Psychiatry/Vol 30, pp.118

Sass, L., Byron, G., (2015), Self- Disturbance And The Bizarre: On Incomprehensibility

In Schizophrenic Delusions, Psychopathology, 48. pp. 293-300 DOI

101159/000437210

Schafer, I., and Fisher, H., Childhood Trauma & Psychosis-What Is the Evidence

Scopophobia .(nd) in Free Dictionary retrieved from Medical dictionary. The Free

Dictionary. com/scopophobia Shakespeare, W., (1623) As You Like It, Act II,

Scene VII

Smith M. and Segal, J (2017) Schizophrenia Symptoms, Signs, & Coping Tips,

HELPGUIDE.ORG, pp.1

Taylor, E.H. (1987), The Biological Basis of Schizophrenia, Social Work, 32(2), pp.115

Vandenbos, G.R. (2000) Schizophrenia. In Encyclopedia of Psychology, (Vol. 7, pp. 160-

163)

Washington D.C.: American Psychological Association, Oxford University Press, pp.

161.

YEN, C., LI, C.Y., YANG, Y-Y., Correlation of Panic Attacks and Hostility in Chronic

Schizophrenia, Psychiatry and Clinical Neurosciences, 55, pp.

Zou, H., Li, Z., Nolan, T.N., Arthur D., Wang, H., HU, L., (2013) Self-Management

Education Interventions

For Persons with Schizophrenia, International Journal of Mental Health Nursing 22, pp.

256-271 Doi: 10.1111/j.14447-0349.2012.00863

About the diagram:

Schizophrenia is delusion! Delusion is to believe that which is not true about others, even when you have been presented with superior evidence to the contrary! I have made up a diagram that gives what I believe to be a very "right on" and "accurate" description of the thought process that one could be said to be experiencing during the entrance of delusion. This diagram I believe to really reflect a true understanding of what is going on in the mind of someone while they are experiencing thoughts that lead to delusion. If one were to put this particular version of this diagram- that highlights the delusion of reference in particular, as a visual aid to help educate just anyone on this issue that it could and should lead to the reduction of delusional thinking among the masses. That's right, if this diagram ever got in the hands of the masses in a "big way" again this should significantly help to stop delusion in man! . I honestly think that the rational alternative that this diagram offers in this instead of being deceived by one's own imagination is clearly presented; and since no one really wants to be a kltutz, or outside looking in their own right mind, the positive effect that I wish that this diagram to have in literally overcoming delusion should take place. My hope and dream is of course that this really happens!

Enclosed is a copy of the diagram itself to cut out and use as visual aid to others that have problems with their nerves of this kind and that could just about be all of us on a bad day I'm afraid if were not careful! Let's learn to be patient and tolerant in everyday life and not to be quick to judge others when it is not in order! Delusion is a bummer! Bad assumption is a bummer too! Attribution is of course terrible, and we don't want it at all, either! Please if you plan on keeping this diagram be responsible enough to know the basic facts too about schizophrenia itself that makes for a truly competent understanding of this disorder! Be good, and may God Bless you and make his face to shine upon you, Amen!

Please cut below:

The diagram:

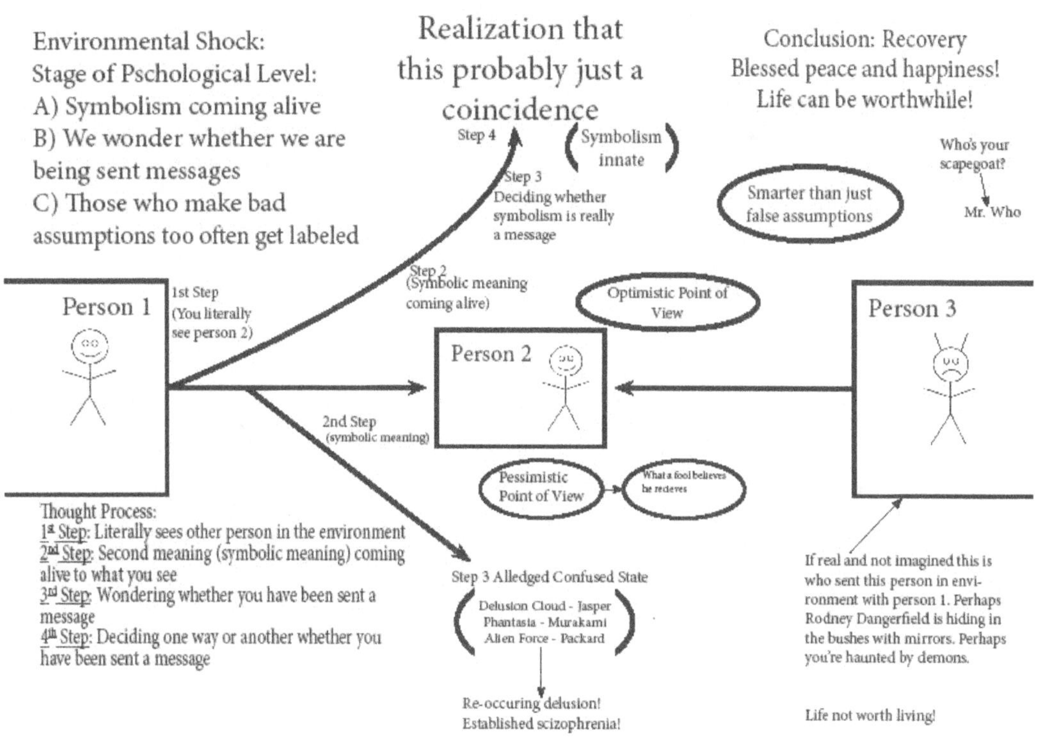
